Esperanza Rising

by
Pam Muñoz Ryan

Teacher Guide

Written by
Veda Boyd Jones

Edited by
Darna McGinnis

Note

The Scholastic Press hardback edition of the book, published by Scholastic, Inc., ©2000 was used to prepare this guide. The page references may differ in other editions.

Please note: Please assess the appropriateness of this book for the age level and maturity of your students prior to reading and discussing it with your class.

ISBN 978-1-58130-786-3

Copyright infringement is a violation of Federal Law.

© 2003, 2004, 2008 by Novel Units, Inc., Bulverde, Texas. All rights reserved. No part of this publication may be reproduced, translated, stored in a retrieval system, or transmitted in any way or by any means (electronic, mechanical, photocopying, recording, or otherwise) without prior written permission from Novel Units, Inc.

Photocopying of student worksheets by a classroom teacher at a non-profit school who has purchased this publication for his/her own class is permissible. Reproduction of any part of this publication for an entire school or for a school system, by for-profit institutions and tutoring centers, or for commercial sale is strictly prohibited.

Novel Units is a registered trademark of Novel Units, Inc.

Printed in the United States of America.

To order, contact your local school supply store, or—

Novel Units, Inc.
P.O. Box 97
Bulverde, TX 78163-0097

Web site: www.novelunits.com

Table of Contents

Summary 3

About the Author 3

Characters 3

Initiating Activities 4

Vocabulary Activities 5

Thirteen Sections 11
    Each section contains: Summary, Vocabulary,
    Discussion Questions, and Supplementary Activities

Post-reading Discussion Questions 29

Post-reading Extension Activities 30

Assessment 31

Skills and Strategies

Thinking
Interpreting, evidence, compare/contrast, forming opinions, identifying stereotypes, paradox, pros/cons, research

Comprehension
Cause/effect, classifying, details, generalizing, inferencing, main idea, predicting, summarizing

Listening/Speaking
Discussion, interview, music, oral report, role-playing

Vocabulary
Compound words, context clues, Spanish words

Writing
Article, description, editorial, poem, list, narrative, letter, report

Literary Elements
Analogy, characterization, descriptions, foreshadowing, plot development, setting, point of view, simile, theme, personification

Across the Curriculum
Art—architecture, crocheting, doll making, drawing; Music—dance, recording; Science—agriculture, fire safety, weather; Social Studies—maps, culture, history, politics, religion; Math—survey statistics

Genre: young adult fiction

Setting: the fictional El Rancho de las Rosas near Aguascalientes, Mexico; migrant camps near Bakersfield, California

Point of View: third-person

Themes: coming of age, differences in society, starting over, first love, accepting change

Conflict: self vs. self, self vs. society

Style: narrative

Date of First Publication: 2000

Summary

Esperanza Rising is set in the 1930s depression era. Esperanza has lived a life of privilege on El Rancho de las Rosas near Aguascalientes, Mexico, until shortly before her thirteenth birthday when her father is killed by bandits. To stay together, Esperanza and her mother are forced to flee to the United States. They escape with their former hired hands, live in a migrant camp near Bakersfield, California, and work in the packing sheds as different crops are harvested. Through threatened labor strikes and her mother's illness, Esperanza learns not to fear starting over.

About the Author

Pam Muñoz Ryan was born in Bakersfield, California, on Christmas Day, 1951. She is the author of over 20 books for young people including *Riding Freedom*. *Esperanza Rising* is based on Ryan's maternal grandmother's story of leaving a life of privilege in Mexico for a quite different life in the United States. The book won the Pura Belpre Medal and the Jane Addams Peace Award, was named an ALA Top Ten Best Book for Young Adults, an America's Award Honor Book, and was a finalist for the *Los Angeles Times* Book Prize. Ryan currently lives 30 miles north of San Diego, California, with her husband, four children, and a couple of dogs in a house that is six blocks from the Pacific Ocean.

Major Characters

Esperanza Ortega: young girl born to a life of privilege in Mexico who becomes poor in the United States

Mama (Ramona Ortega): Esperanza's mother

Abuelita: Esperanza's grandmother

Hortensia: housekeeper at the Ortega's ranch in Mexico and a migrant worker in the United States

Alfonso: Hortensia's husband, the Ortega ranch foreman until he moves to the United States

Miguel: son of Hortensia and Alfonso, and Esperanza's childhood friend

Isabel: Miguel's cousin who lives at the migrant camp

Marta: American citizen who leads the strikers

Minor Characters

Tío Luis and Tío Marco: Esperanza's uncles (her father's step-brothers)

Marisol: Esperanza's close friend in Mexico

Señor Rodríguez: Marisol's father

Juan and Josefina: Alfonso's brother and sister-in-law who live in a migrant camp

Initiating Activities

Choose one or more of the following activities to establish an appropriate mindset before reading the novel.

1. Multi-media: Show videotapes, pictures, and photographs that depict ranches in 1930s Mexico. Check out several books about Mexico and the revolution to have as resources throughout the study of the novel. Also have articles, books, and pictures of migrant farms in California during the Depression era. Allow each student to look at a resource item for three minutes before passing it on to the next person. Continue passing resources around until students have seen most of the resources. Seeing pictures of the sheds, fields, cabins, and tents of the migrant camps will give them background knowledge for the novel.

2. Geography/Culture: Show a map of Mexico and locate Aguascalientes. Research what life was like for the privileged and what it was like for the peasants during the time period the novel depicts. Give vital statistics about Mexico, its population, language, religion, crops, and history. Show the Mexican flag.

3. Geography/History: Show a map of the United States and locate Bakersfield. Explain what life was like for migrant workers who moved up and down the coast following the harvest.

4. Math: Give statistics about the Depression, unemployment numbers, and mention the Great Dust Bowl in Oklahoma that led to Oklahomans moving to California in search of jobs.

5. Allusions: Read the myth of the phoenix to the class so they will understand a later reference to the myth and the novel's title.

6. Discussion: Show a picture of workers walking a picket line and discuss what strikers hope to gain by a work stoppage.

7. Predicting: Give students the following clues and have them write a paragraph predicting what they think will happen in the story: funeral, escape, migrant camp, work ethic, loneliness, illness, mountains and valleys, reunion, love, change.

Vocabulary Activities

1. Spanish Vocabulary: As they read the novel, have students write each Spanish word that is defined in the text on a 3x5 card along with its definition. Give them each an envelope to store the cards. During the unit, have them periodically use the cards as flash cards to familiarize themselves with the book's Spanish words.

2. Vocabulary Sort: Have students sort vocabulary words into categories (e.g., nouns, verbs, adjectives, and adverbs).

3. Sentences: Have students select three or four vocabulary words and use them in one sentence. They may do this with the vocabulary lists for each chapter.

4. Words Maps: Have students complete word maps for vocabulary words. For example: vicious (8), devious (33), unpredictable (51), blustery (64), vigorously (114), grotto (123), roil (147), cavernous (168), susceptible (183), animated (198), despondent (207), optimism (224), obsessed (244).

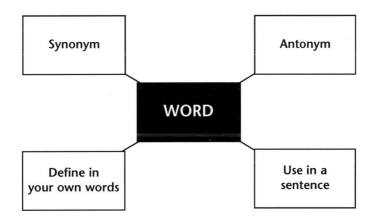

5. Context Clues: Remind students of the various types of context clues such as description, example, synonym, contrast, and comparison. Examples of words from the novel to practice using context clue strategies include: scythe (4), premonition (9), silhouetted (41) monotonous (72), brooded (99), regimented (153), bereft (168), menacing (200).

6. Prefix Hints: Have students identify the target vocabulary words with prefixes and categorize them. Examples from the novel: in—indignation (30), indebted (52) and infinite (251); un—unpredictable (51), unrelenting (116).

7. Vocabulary Charades: Have students act out some of the vocabulary words that deal with behavior and have other students guess which ones they are. Examples: vicious (8), capricious (13), irritable (73), humiliation (117), frantically (145), depressed (162), animated (198), infuriated (244).

8. Visual Images: Have students use an encyclopedia, the Internet, or other resources to find pictures of vocabulary words related to specific categories. Examples include: Botany—arbors (1), tendril (1), scythe (4), rosehip (35), smudge pot (179); Religious—rosaries (26), alms (66), cherubs (88), La Navidad (172), nativity (173), novena (214).

9. Word Map—Verb: Have students complete word maps for the vocabulary verbs. For example: pervaded (38), undulating (68), brooded (99), smirked (99), riveted (177).

Word Map for a Verb

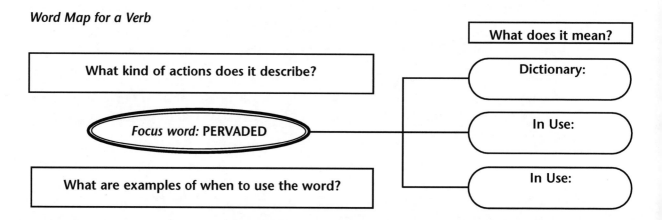

10. Sentences: Have students choose words from the vocabulary lists and write a sentence about the main character using each word and then write a sentence about themselves using the same words. For example: pretentious (33), unpredictable (51), groggily (85), gingerly (114), peculiar (146), despondent (207).

Using Predictions

We all make predictions as we read—little guesses about what will happen next, how a conflict will be resolved, which details will be important to the plot, which details will help fill in our sense of a character. Students should be encouraged to predict, to make sensible guesses as they read the novel.

As students work on their predictions, these discussion questions can be used to guide them: What are some of the ways to predict? What is the process of a sophisticated reader's thinking and predicting? What clues does an author give to help us make predictions? Why are some predictions more likely to be accurate than others?

Create a chart for recording predictions. This could be either an individual or class activity. As each subsequent chapter is discussed, students can review and correct their previous predictions about plot and characters as necessary.

- Use the facts and ideas the author gives.
- Use your own prior knowledge.
- Apply any new information (i.e., from class discussion) that may cause you to change your mind.

Predictions
_____
_____
_____
_____

Prediction Chart

What characters have we met so far?	What is the conflict in the story?	What are your predictions?	Why did you make those predictions?

Character Analysis

Directions: The names of some of the characters who appear in the novel are written in the boxes below. Begin the chart after reading pages 1–22 and add to the chart as you continue reading the novel. Working in small groups, discuss the attributes of the various characters with other members of your group. In each character's box, write several words or phrases you feel describe him or her.

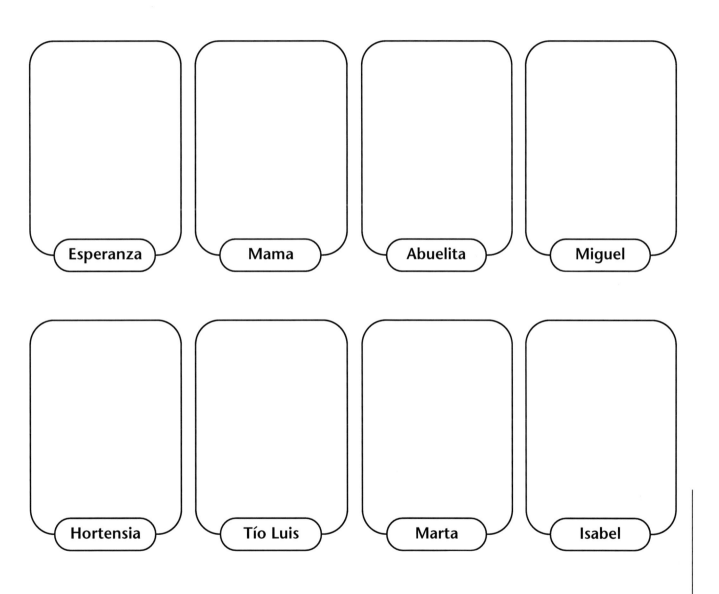

Graphing Plot Lines

Characters

Setting

Problem

- Climax
- Resolution
- Building Action
- Beginning

Aguascalientes, Mexico and Las Uvas, pp. 1–22

The preface introduces Papa and six-year-old Esperanza in 1924. The father and daughter are walking through the vineyard, and Papa tells Esperanza that if she lies down, she can hear the heartbeat of the land. She listens and finally hears the heartbeat of the land combined with Papa's and her own.

In the second chapter, Esperanza begins the grape harvest by cutting the first bunch. At the end of the three-week harvest will be her thirteenth birthday and a big fiesta. She dreams of the time when she will have her presentation party. She remembers that at one time she wanted to marry Miguel, but her mother explained that a "big river" separates the landowners from the hired workers. Esperanza recalls how, when she told this to Miguel, their relationship changed from friends to acquaintances. Esperanza pricks her finger on a rose thorn, which foreshadows something painful to come. Miguel and his father find Papa and bring his body home.

Vocabulary

arbors (1)	tendril (1)	scythe (4)	vicious (8)
premonition (9)	serenaded (9)	congregate (9)	porcelain (9)
adobe (10)	crochet (12)	distinguished (13)	nape (13)
capricious (13)	propriety (13)	philosophical (13)	resurrected (16)
dwindled (21)	transforming (21)	candelabra (21)	

Discussion Questions

1. What does the introductory information tell us about the story? *(It gives setting, time, and shows the relationship between Papa and Esperanza. Answers will vary. p. 1)*

2. Why do you think the land is important? Do you think it will play a part in the rest of the story? *(Papa's eyes dance with love for the land and he says it is alive and has a heartbeat. Answers will vary. p. 1)*

3. Is it important that Esperanza hears not only the land's heartbeat but also her father's and her own? Why? *(Yes; Esperanza needs to feel that she, her father, and the land are all connected. Answers will vary. pp 2–3)*

4. Why is it unusual for a female to cut the first grape cluster? *(This honor is usually reserved for the eldest son. p. 4)*

5. Explain the "big river" metaphor that separates Esperanza and Miguel. *(They are from different social classes and will never be able to associate with each other, and especially not get married. p. 18)*

6. No one says in words that Papa is dead (p. 22). Discuss how the characters express their feelings. *(Answers will vary.)*

7. **Prediction:** Abulelita says there is no rose without thorns. How does this saying predict what's to come in the story? *(It means there is no life without difficulties. Papa's death begins Esperanza's life of difficulties. p. 14)*

Supplementary Activities

1. Social Studies: Have students locate Aguascalientes, Mexico, on a map. Let them guess where the fictional El Rancho de las Rosas should be.

2. Literary Analysis/Symbols: The heartbeat of the land symbolizes agriculture in the book. Have students begin a list of other symbols that occur in the book.

3. Literary Analysis/Characterization: Have students begin a character analysis chart (see page 9 of this guide) for Esperanza, Mama (Ramona), and Abuelita.

4. Literary Analysis/Plot Development: Have students begin a plot graph (see page 10 of this guide) to use as they read this story.

5. Social Studies: Have students research the Mexican revolution of 1920 and make a chart of the leaders on each side.

6. Social Studies: Instead of chapter numbers, the author has named each chapter after a fruit or vegetable. Have the students begin a list of the foods and add to it as they read each chapter. Have them write a sentence explaining the significance of each food to the story.

7. Science: Have the students research the way grapes used to be harvested by hand and compare it to how grapes are now harvested by machine.

8. Literary Analysis/Similes: The author uses similes that compare characters to animals—Alfonso looks like a forlorn puppy (p. 16), and the two uncles look like underfed billy goats (p. 19). Have students bring a picture of a person from a magazine or newspaper and describe the person using an animal comparison. Have the students begin a list of similes and add to the list as they read.

9. Writing: Abuelita quotes an old proverb, "There is no rose without thorns," which means that life has difficulties (p. 14). Have students find a familiar proverb and write a few sentences about its meaning.

10. Language: Have the students begin a list of Spanish words that are defined in the text and add to the list as they read the book.

Las Papayas, pp. 23–38

Esperanza must break the news of her father's death to Señor Rodríguez. The three-day funeral observance is finally over, and the family gathers for the reading of the will. Papa leaves the house, its contents, and the revenue from the grape harvest to Mama and Esperanza. According to Mexican tradition, women do not own land, so he leaves the land to his brother, Luis. Luis proposes marriage to Mama, who refuses. Luis gives her overnight to change her mind or he threatens to make life very difficult for her. Esperanza talks to Miguel, who says his family will go to the United States instead of working for Luis, who is a corrupt man.

Vocabulary

anguish (23)	rosaries (26)	indignation (30)	pretentious (33)
devious (33)	rosehip (35)	throttle (35)	pervaded (38)

Discussion Questions

1. What prompts Esperanza to remember the events of the night before? *(She is in Papa's bed. p. 23)*

2. Why do Esperanza and her friend Marisol act differently when alone than when with others at the funeral? *(While with adults, they have refined manners, but when by themselves, they hold hands and cry. Answers will vary about cause. p. 26)*

3. Why does Esperanza delay opening her gifts? *(They remind her of the fiesta that she was supposed to have. p. 27)*

4. Why does Esperanza react to the doll the way she does? *(Answers will vary).*

5. What is left to Esperanza and her mother in the will? Do you think this will be enough for them to live on? Why? *(They own the house and its contents and will receive a yearly income from the grapes. Answers will vary. p. 30)*

6. Why is Esperanza so shocked at the marriage proposal? How would you feel if you were in Esperanza's place? How would you feel in her mother's place? *(Answers will vary).*

7. What does Tío Luis really want from Ramona? *(He wants her influence so he can be elected governor. p. 33)*

8. **Prediction:** As their landlord, what can Tío Luis do to Esperanza and her mother? *(Answers will vary. p. 32)*

9. **Prediction:** After Esperanza and Miguel talk in the garden, why are Miguel's eyes full of hurt? *(She has pulled away from him, and he misinterprets her action. Answers may vary. p. 37)*

Supplementary Activities

1. Literary Analysis/Characterization: Have students add characteristics to the character analysis chart about Tío Luis and Miguel.

2. Literary Analysis/Predictions: Have students begin a prediction chart (see page 8 of this guide).

3. **Literary Analysis/Descriptive Language:** Point out the author's use of creative language to describe feelings such as "a heavy blanket of anguish smothered her smallest joy" (p. 23), "Or was her heart weighing her down?" (p. 24), and "she watched the grief twist Señor Rodríguez's face" (p. 25). Have students use their own descriptive language to describe sad and happy feelings.

4. **Social Studies:** Have the students research the funeral customs in Mexico in 1930 and compare them with funeral customs in the United States at that same time.

5. **Math:** Have the students ask five adults if they have drawn up wills. Add all the student answers together for a larger statistical sampling, convert it to a percentage, and discuss the outcome of the survey.

Los Higos, pp. 39–57

Esperanza awakens to the house on fire. The family escapes, but the house, the stables, and the vineyard are burned. They suspect the uncles of setting the fire. Miguel's family decides to move to the United States where his uncle is working. Although she tells Tío Luis that she will marry him, Mama is just buying time until she and Esperanza can plan their escape. Abuelita is temporarily staying with her sisters, who are nuns. She says she will join them when her health improves.

Vocabulary

silhouetted (41)	salvage (43)	mortars and pestles (43)	phoenix (50)
unpredictable (51)	indebted (52)	valise (55)	charred (56)
venom (57)			

Discussion Questions

1. Why doesn't the family talk about what started the fire? *(There is no need because they all believe the uncles have arranged it. p. 43)*

2. With her inheritance gone, what are Mama's options? Do you agree or disagree that these are her only choices? *(She can marry Tío Luis or she must leave the area, and it would be better if she goes far away. Answers will vary. pp. 46–47)*

3. If Mama marries Tío Luis, what will happen to Esperanza? *(She will be sent to boarding school. p. 45)*

4. What does Abuelita's advice to her granddaughter mean? What does Abuelita want Esperanza to learn from the advice? *("Do not be afraid to start over." Answers will vary. p. 49)*

5. Why did everyone laugh when Esperanza says she can also work? *(Answers will vary. p. 50)*

6. Mama tells Tío Luis that they need a wagon to visit Abuelita, but what is the real reason? *(Answers will vary. p. 54)*

7. With all that has happened to them, Esperanza is surprised that her mother is concerned with a poor family who needs clothes, and she is doubly surprised to learn that the clothes are for

Esperanza and her mother. What does this say about Esperanza? What does it say about her mother? *(Answers will vary.)*

8. **Prediction:** What does Mama tell Esperanza about Papa when they leave the ranch in the dead of night? What does this mean and how will it occur in the story? *("Papa's heart will find us wherever we go." Answers will vary. p. 56)*

Supplementary Activities

1. Literary Analysis/Characterization: Have students add characteristics to the character analysis chart about Miguel and Hortensia.

2. Science: Esperanza and her mother put wet cloths over their faces and crouch down to flee the fire (pp. 40–41), and Alfonso rolls Miguel over when his back is on fire. Discuss fire safety and have the students write basic safety rules.

3. Research: Have the students find the various charitable organizations in their areas that give clothes to the poor.

Las Guayabas, pp. 58–80

Esperanza, her mother, and Hortensia hide under a fake floor in the wagon for the two-day journey to the train station. Esperanza can't believe she and her mother must ride with peasants in a dirty train car. Although her mother befriends other riders, Esperanza distances herself from them. She witnesses a peasant giving a coin to a beggar, and Miguel tells her the poor help those with less while the rich help only the rich. He tells her the more Spanish blood there is in a person in Mexico, the richer they are because their complexions are lighter.

Vocabulary

renegades (61) persistent (62) blustery (64) spewing (66)
alms (66) undulating (68) monotonous (72) irritable (73)
caboose (76) complexions (79)

Discussion Questions

1. How is the wagon altered for the escape? Does this seem like a good plan? What will they do if they are discovered? *(The men build a floor on top of the wagon bed with room between the two for the women to hide. They put guavas on the top floor so observers will think they are farmers transporting fruit to market. Answers will vary. pp. 58-60)*

2. How does the train ride that Esperanza took with Papa differ from the train ride she is taking with Mama? *(The train ride with Papa was first class with leather seats and a dining car with white linens, crystal, and silver. Mama and Esperanza sit in a dirty car with peasants on wooden benches. pp. 64, 66)*

3. Why doesn't Esperanza allow the barefoot girl to hold the doll? What does this say about Esperanza? *(The doll is special, and the dirty girl would have soiled it. Answers will vary. p. 70)*

4. Why is Esperanza annoyed with Alfonso? *(He will not tell her what is in the bag that he soaks with water at each train stop. p. 73)*

5. What does Mama say when Esperanza chastises her for confiding her personal business to a peasant? What do you think of Esperanza for talking like this to her mother? *("...now we are peasants, too." Answers will vary. p. 77)*

6. Mama tells Esperanza that they can't afford a first class car and that they are peasants now. Why can't Esperanza understand her position? *(Answers will vary. p. 67, 77)*

7. What is the significance of the roadside shrines that Esperanza sees? *(Someone was killed at that spot. pp. 68–69)*

8. **Prediction:** What is in Alfonso's bag? *(Answers will vary. p. 73)*

9. **Prediction:** Will Esperanza's Spanish blood help her in the United States? *(Answers will vary. pp. 79–80)*

Supplementary Activities

1. Literary Analysis/Foreshadowing: Introduce the concept of foreshadowing that writers use to give the reader a glimpse of what may happen. Recall the foreshadowing of Tío Luis' threat (p. 32) and of Alfonso's bag (p. 73). Instruct students to keep a list of other examples of foreshadowing.

2. Social Studies: On a map of Mexico, have the students find the town of Zacatecas.

3. Research: Have the students find pictures of different types of passenger train cars in the 1930s.

4. Art: Have one child read aloud the instructions for making a yarn doll (p. 71), and have two other students make the doll with input from the other students.

5. Writing: Have students write journal entries for an imaginary four-day train journey.

Los Melones, pp. 81–99

The train arrives in Mexicali, and the group must pass through immigration. Although their papers are in order, it takes some time for Mama and Esperanza to be waved through. They climb on another train that takes them to Los Angeles. Here they are met by Miguel's extended family and are taken to the Mexican camp of migrant workers. On the way, they pick up a couple of girls who are walking to the camp. Esperanza and one girl, Marta, have cross words when Marta accuses Esperanza of being "a princess who's come to be a peasant" (p. 96).

Vocabulary

panorama (81)	immigration (81)	stagnant (81)	groggily (85)
jalopy (88)	cherubs (88)	sparse (90)	arroyo (91)
staggered (93)	cascade (93)	Filipinos (97)	brooded (99)
smirked (99)			

Discussion Questions

1. How does Mama treat the immigration officer? What does this say about Mama? *(She speaks calmly as if he were a servant. Answers will vary. p. 82)*

2. Why are some people being sent back on the train to Mexico? What would you choose to do if you were in this situation? *(Some have no papers or false ones. If there is a problem with one member of a family, the entire family might choose to return instead of being separated. Answers will vary. pp. 83–84)*

3. Describe the ride in the truck. What is Esperanza's reaction to this trip? Why? *(Juan, Josefina, Mama, and Hortensia ride in the front of the old truck. In the truck bed sits all the kids and Alfonso. Esperanza sits with her back against the cab. Alfonso makes a canopy against the sun by tying an old blanket to the wooden side slats. Answers will vary. pp. 87–88)*

4. In what language will Isabel learn to read? Why does Esperanza think that learning to read is such a little thing? *(English; Answers will vary. p. 89)*

5. What level of schooling has Esperanza attained? Do you think she speaks English? *(She has completed level eight in private school and is ready for high school. Answers will vary. p. 89)*

6. What happens to Esperanza as she lays on her back at the picnic? *(She feels as if she is floating, but she faints. p. 92)*

7. Why do people of different nationalities live in different camps? If you were a company owner, would you follow this policy? *(The company doesn't want them banding together to demand higher wages or better living conditions. Answers will vary. p. 98)*

8. Why doesn't Esperanza like Marta? *(Answers will vary.)*

9. **Prediction:** Will Marta and Miguel become good friends? *(Answers will vary.)*

Supplementary Activities

1. Literary Activities/Characterization: Have students add Marta to their character analysis chart.

2. Social Studies: Have students trace the train route on a map of Mexico and California.

3. Social Studies: Have the students compare the weather at the ranch to the weather in Los Angeles.

4. Writing: The author has written "...her tears worming down her face" (p. 92). Have students write sentences using other animal words as verbs, e.g., snaking, pigging out.

Las Cebollas, pp. 100–120

Esperanza can't believe that so many people will be living in the same cabin, which isn't as nice as servant quarters at the ranch, but is more like the stables. Her job is to care for the children with Isabel while the others pick grapes. Isabel teaches her how to do laundry. When Esperanza attempts to sweep, Marta and other women laugh at her. Miguel teaches her to sweep, and Esperanza makes a deal with Isabel that she'll tell her what it is like to be rich if Isabel will teach her how to do common chores.

Vocabulary

cringed (101)   bestowed (104)   lush (110)   debris (110)
splotches (110) gingerly (114)   murky (114)   vigorously (114)
unrelenting (116) humiliation (117) ridicule (117)

Discussion Questions

1. What does Esperanza think she could learn when Marta jumps out of the truck and talks to some girls? Why does this suddenly become important to her? *(She could learn English. Answers will vary. p. 101)*

2. What does the cabin look like and who will be staying in it? How does this contrast from Esperanza's home in Mexico? Is her reaction what you would expect? *(It has two small rooms. One room has a kitchen and one mattress; the other room has a mattress and a cot. Esperanza, her mother, Isabel, Alfonso, and Hortensia will sleep there. Answers will vary. pp. 102–103)*

3. What are the two choices that Mama says they have? Why does Mama see the obvious choice when Esperanza does not? *(They can choose to be together and miserable, or together and happy. Answers will vary. p. 104)*

4. Why does Mama's braid upset Esperanza? *(In Mexico, she wore her hair up in a plaited bun, and at night she wore it down. A braid seems low class to Esperanza. p. 109)*

5. How could Esperanza tell which type of produce was in the trucks? *(The sharp smell from the shredded outer skins tells her they are onions. p. 110)*

6. Why does Esperanza shake hands with Silvia? *(She doesn't want to hold the dirty hand, but she knows Mama will be disappointed in her if she isn't kind. p. 111)*

7. What does Miguel think is the only thing that Esperanza had learned in Mexico? Do you agree with this? *(how to give orders; Answers will vary. p. 118)*

8. **Prediction:** Will Esperanza learn to do the chores that Isabel thinks are so easy? *(Answers will vary.)*

Supplementary Activities

1. Literary Analysis/Characterization: Have students add Isabel to their character analysis chart. Have them add characteristics to Miguel's chart.

2. Research: Mama says Esperanza is too young to work in the sheds. Have students find out if there was an age requirement for working on farms in the 1930s. The Internet may be a source for this information.

3. Writing: Have students write a paragraph describing how they learned to do a chore.

4. Writing: Have students write a paragraph describing an embarrassing moment.

5. Research: Have students find out which types of produce are grown in their area.

Las Almendras, pp. 121–138

After the first day at work, everyone is tired, including Esperanza. She and her mother are surprised after supper by Miguel and his father, who show them the rose clippings they have planted. In Mexico, they had dug under the burned rose garden and found healthy roots. On Saturday, everyone bathes and cleans up for the jamaica. Esperanza decides to face others and let them laugh at her if they will for her ignorance of how to do chores. At the jamaica, Marta tries to rouse people to strike for better wages and better housing in two weeks during cotton picking time. Esperanza and her mother discuss it after they are home in bed. They plan what they will pray for the next day at church.

Vocabulary

massaged (121)   grotto (123)   mulch (124)   trellis (124)
crimped (125)   burlap (127)   swaddled (131)   litter (131)

Discussion Questions

1. After a hard day's work, Mama starts supper. Why does this surprise Esperanza? Why is Esperanza having such a difficult time understanding their new financial circumstances? How would you accept the change? *(She knows her mother did not cook in Mexico. Answers will vary. p. 121)*

2. Describe the shrine that was built behind the cabin. *(Half an old washtub set on its side formed an arch over a plastic statue of Our Lady of Guadalupe. Rocks were placed around the tub, and a sticks-and-rope fence around a plot of earth protected thorny stems of rose plants. p. 123)*

3. What were the two special roses? Why were they special? Do you think this will have significance in the story? *(The ones Papa had planted for Miguel and Esperanza were planted as well as other slips. Answers will vary. p. 124)*

4. Why has Miguel put a trellis beside Esperanza's rose? What is Miguel trying to tell her by this act? *(so the rose will climb and grow; Answers will vary. p. 124)*

5. How does Esperanza show Hortensia that she is accepting the change in the bathing routine? *(When Hortensia needs hot water for her bath, Esperanza gets it for her. p. 127)*

6. Describe the jamaica. *(Musicians sat on a platform lit with lights. Cloth-covered tables held food for sale. Bingo tables were set up and chairs surrounded the dance area. pp. 129–130)*

7. How does Marta compare the kittens to the workers? Do you think this is an effective way to get people on your side of an issue? If not, how would you address the workers? *(She calls them both "small, meek animals." Answers will vary. p. 132)*

8. **Prediction:** Will the workers strike?

Supplementary Activities

1. Literary Analysis/Descriptive Language: Have the students write a paragraph about Mama's words, "Didn't I tell you that Papa's heart would find us wherever we go?" (p. 125)

2. Literary Analysis/Characterization: Have the students add details to Marta's box in the character analysis chart.

3. Writing: After showing news footage of a demonstration, have the students write a paragraph about their feelings. Did the students feel threatened?

4. Social Studies: Have the students ask their parents about their grandparents and discover how many students have grandparents who immigrated to the United States. Give students the opportunity to share their grandparents' stories.

5. Science: Have the students make a list of the chores they must do when they have a pet that depends on them for its existence.

6. Music: Check out audiocassettes or CDs of Latin music. Discuss the different instruments heard: drum, horns, guitars, accordions. Have the students identify the different instruments in the music.

Las Ciruelas, pp. 139–157

Esperanza's first day is not easy. She burns the beans and feeds plums to the babies, which make them ill. Within several days, Esperanza has a handle on her jobs. When a huge dust storm hits, she gets the babies to the safety of the cabin, but the women are in the open shed, and the men are in the fields. They arrive home covered in dirt and with nasty coughs. Mama's cough gets worse and she becomes ill. The doctor says she has Valley Fever, and if she survives, it will take six months to get her strength back.

Vocabulary

concerns (139)	frantically (145)	peculiar (146)	roil (147)
encrusted (151)	spasm (151)	suede (152)	regimented (153)
bustling (153)	contagious (156)	immunized (156)	

Discussion Questions

1. What instructions does Isabel give Esperanza about getting the babies to sleep? Is this a good plan? How would you handle having two babies to care for? *(Wait until Pepe is down and asleep, then put Lupe down or they will play and not go to sleep. Answers will vary. p. 139)*

2. What goes wrong on Esperanza's first day in charge of the babies? Why does she react as she does to these domestic disasters? *(She feeds them plums, which make them ill, and she burns the beans. Answers will vary. p. 141)*

3. What conditions forewarn the workers of the dust storm? Why does Esperanza not understand what is coming? *(The sky is tinged with yellow and the air is full of static. She's never experienced one before. p. 146)*

4. What is the goal of those workers who want to strike and those who do not wish to strike? Which side would you be on? Why? *(They both want to feed their families. Answers will vary. p. 146)*

5. Describe the dust storm. *(The wind blows dust so hard that it pits everything it hits, and dust fills the air until it diminishes visibility. pp. 148–149)*

6. What is Valley Fever? *(It's a lung disease caused by dust spores. p. 155)*

7. **Prediction:** Will Mama survive the disease? Defend your answer. *(Answers will vary.)*

Supplementary Activities

1. Literary Analysis/Characterization: Have students add to Mama's section of their characterization chart.

2. Science: Have students research dust storms and find where they are prevalent in the United States.

3. Writing: Have students write a paragraph about an experience babysitting a child.

Las Papas, pp. 158-178

Esperanza nurses Mama, but she does not get better and calls out for Abuelita. Esperanza crochets on the blanket that Abuelita had started long ago. The doctor arrives weeks later and says that Mama should be in the hospital. Mama is depressed and very weak. With Mama in the hospital, Esperanza must find work. She works in the shed cutting potato eyes. She listens to talk about the strike that may take place in the spring when picking season comes again. On Christmas, Esperanza takes a stone as a present to Mama, but Mama never wakes to see it.

Vocabulary

depressed (162)	shawl (164)	tule (167)	penetrating (167)
rumbled (168)	bereft (168)	frigid (168)	cavernous (168)
repatriation (170)	La Navidad (172)	Advent (173)	nativity (173)
incense (174)	frayed (174)	ritual (176)	poinsettia (177)
rhinestone (177)	riveted (177)		

Discussion Questions

1. Sometimes an author uses sentence fragments for emphasis. What do these fragments emphasize? "As it had found its way into Mama's lungs." *(The dust infiltrates everything. p.159)* "And the faintest scent of peppermint." *(This was Abuelita's scent. p. 159)* "Because she was wishing that Mama would not die." *(This wish is what Esperanza wove into the blanket. p.161)*

2. Why does Esperanza feel as she does about the mountains and valleys in the blanket? *(She thinks of them as high points and low points of her life, especially the valley of Mama's sickness. p. 160)*

3. How does the author show time passage during Mama's sickness? *("The fields frosted over" shows time passing. Christmas arrives. pp. 162, 176)*

4. Why does Esperanza go to work? What would you do in her situation? *(She must pay doctor bills and earn money to bring Abuelita to Mama. Answers will vary. p. 165)*

5. What does Esperanza wear to the shed? Why do the others lend her the clothes? *(She wears all she could borrow: old wool pants, a sweater, a jacket, a cap and thick gloves over thin gloves. Answers will vary. p. 167)*

6. How do the women feel about the proposed strike? *(Answers will vary. pp. 170–171)*

7. What does Isabel mean by saying she wants "anything" for Christmas? *(Answers will vary. p. 175)*

8. **Prediction:** Will Esperanza get what she wants for Christmas? *(Answers will vary.)*

Supplementary Activities

1. Writing: Have the students write a paragraph about a gift that they gave or received that had special meaning.

2. Writing: Esperanza looks around the cabin and describes it. Have the students write a paragraph describing their classroom.

3. Social Studies: Have the students research what it takes for an immigrant to become an American citizen.

4. Literary Analysis/Personification: Discuss things to which the author gives human traits. Examples: "trucks could not find their way" (p. 150 from earlier chapter), "hopeful color" (p. 161). Have the students make their own list of personifications.

Los Aguacates, pp. 179-198

Esperanza works tying up grapevines. She misses her mother, and when her mother develops pneumonia, Esperanza can't even go to the hospital because she might carry in a germ. Esperanza goes with Miguel to the market. She buys groceries, a money order, and a piñata for Mama. On the way home, they give a ride to Marta and her mother. Esperanza gives away the piñata and some food to a hungry family. Marta warns them of an impending strike when the asparagus is ready. Because of strikers quitting jobs, Miguel gets a job with the railroad.

Vocabulary

vapors (179)	smudge pot (179)	pruning (180)	taut (180)
pulp (180)	glycerin (180)	mesquite (181)	suppleness (181)
weathered (182)	susceptible (183)	strewn (183)	bedraggled (183)
loamy (186)	piñatas (189)	migrant (192)	twinge (192)
rutted (192)	humanity (193)	hypnotized (194)	squalor (194)
animated (198)			

Discussion Questions

1. What is the hand-softening recipe that Esperanza uses? Why does this work? *(She mixes avocado pulp and glycerin and puts it on her hands for 20 minutes. Answers will vary. pp. 180–181)*

2. Why is Esperanza barred from seeing her mother? Why does she feel as she does about this? *(She could bring in germs. Answers will vary. p. 183)*

3. Why do the Mexicans shop at Mr. Yakota's store? Is this smart salesmanship? Why? *(He treats them kindly unlike others who think of them as uneducated. Answers will vary. pp. 186–187)*

4. Why does Esperanza buy the piñata for Mama? What does it say about Esperanza that she gives it away? *(Mama will know she's thinking of her. Answers will vary. p. 190)*

5. Why does Marta warn Esperanza and Miguel about the strike? *(Answers will vary. pp. 194–196)*

6. What is the family celebrating when they have breakfast foods for supper? *(Miguel is hired in the railroad machine shop. p. 197)*

7. **Prediction:** Esperanza thinks of her mother and grandmother and knows what she must do about the strike. What is it? *(Answers will vary.)*

Supplementary Activities

1. Literary Analysis: Have students add to their list of foods mentioned in the book. Have them write a sentence telling about the food and its significance to the story.

2. Literary Analysis: Have students add to their list of symbols used in the book.

3. Writing: Esperanza missed the simple things about her mother. Have students list five things they would miss if they couldn't see someone in their family for a month.

4. **Research:** Have students research how money orders are bought and how they can be exchanged for money.

5. **Writing:** Have students bring in a picture from a magazine of someone unfamiliar. Then, have the students write a one-paragraph description of the person. Discuss how we often judge people by appearance rather than character.

Los Espárragos, pp. 199-213

Esperanza defies a picket line and marches to the shed to pack asparagus. Strikers put surprises in the harvest for the packers to find: snakes, rats, and razorblades. Only when immigration officials make a sweep do the chanting on the lines stop. Esperanza protects Marta from the officials. The next day she asks Miguel to drive her by the strikers' farm to find Marta, but the place is deserted. She sees the remnants of the piñata.

Vocabulary

menacing (200)   shards (202)   caravan (205)   deportation (207)
despondent (207)

Discussion Questions

1. What do the strikers do to organize? *(They hand out flyers and paint slogans on barns. p. 199)*

2. What type of surprises do the strikers slip under the asparagus? Are these ploys effective? *(Workers find rats, snakes, razor blades, and shards of glass among the asparagus. Answers will vary. p. 202)*

3. What is voluntary deportment? Would you get on the bus if your mother were on it? *(When the bus leaves with the captured Mexicans so that other family members will join them instead of being separated. Answers will vary. p. 297)*

4. Why doesn't Esperanza tell the others about Marta hiding? What does this say about Esperanza's character? *(She doesn't want to separate Marta from her mother. Answers will vary. p. 208)*

5. How does Esperanza help Marta avoid detection by immigration officials? Would you have done the same thing? Why? *(She gives her an apron and some asparagus and tells her to disguise herself as a worker. Answers will vary. p. 209)*

6. Why does Miguel think that the strikers will be back? *(Answers will vary. p. 210)*

7. Why is the strikers' farm deserted? *(Immigration has been there, too. p. 212)*

8. **Prediction:** Will Marta find her mother? *(Answers will vary.)*

Supplementary Activities

1. Social Studies: Have the students read about picket lines and their significance to strikes.

2. Literary Analysis/Characterization: Have the students add to Marta's characterization chart.

3. Social Studies: Have the students use the Internet to learn about the life of Cesar Chavez, who organized the farm workers.

4. Literary Analysis/Similes: Have the students add to their lists of similes: "like a mass of marbles that had already been hit" (p. 205). Have the students write similes to describe the silence (p. 204).

5. Writing: Have the students write a paragraph describing a place that's been deserted—a playground, a park, an old house, a ball field.

6. Social Studies/Maps: Have the students look at their maps of California and Mexico and trace a likely route for the immigration buses to take strikers to Mexico.

Los Duraznos, pp. 214-233

Esperanza finds Isabel praying at the shine. Isabel wants desperately to be the Queen of the May on May Day. Esperanza learns that a new camp is being made for Oklahomans. These people will get old barracks with hot water and inside bathrooms. She is outraged. She and Miguel have words, and she tells him he is still a peasant. Miguel leaves in the night for northern California. Isabel isn't the queen, but Esperanza gives her the doll she'd received for her birthday. Mama is released from the hospital. Esperanza intends to show Mama the money orders she's been saving, but they are gone.

Vocabulary

novena (214)   barracks (218)   whooshing (223)   prophecy (224)
optimism (224)   diplomas (229)   relapse (229)

Discussion Questions

1. Why does Esperanza feel that Isabel will not be chosen queen? *(A Mexican has never been chosen, no matter how high her grades. p. 216)*

2. How does Esperanza react to learning that Mexicans get to swim in the Oklahoma camp swimming pool only on Friday afternoons before the pool is cleaned on Saturday morning? Are her feelings justified? *(Answers will vary.)*

3. Why is Miguel's job changed at the railroad? Are Miguel's feelings about this consistent with his character? Why? *(Oklahoma men took the mechanic jobs, so he had to dig ditches or lay tracks. Answers will vary. p. 219)*

4. Why does Esperanza throw the dough against the wall? Does this action relieve her frustrations? Does this type of reaction help you deal with frustrations? *(She is frustrated by the injustices against the Mexicans: the queen ordeal, the Oklahoma camp, and Miguel's job. Answers will vary. p. 220)*

5. Miguel says that Esperanza has never lived without hope, but he has. Why? *(Answers will vary. He could never cross the class system in Mexico, which left him without hope. Esperanza has hope in this new land, even though she feels she's fighting an uphill battle. p. 222)*

6. Why does Esperanza say that Miguel is still a second-class citizen? Do you agree with Esperanza or with Miguel? Why? *(She thinks he lets the boss take advantage of him. Answers will vary. p. 222)*

7. Why does Miguel believe Esperanza still thinks she is a queen? *(Answers will vary. She tells him she has lost everything and all she was meant to be. She also calls him a peasant. p. 224)*

8. Why does Esperanza give the doll to Isabel? What does this reveal about how Esperanza has changed? *(She wants her to feel better about not being queen, and the doll will last more than one day, unlike being queen. Answers will vary. p. 227)*

9. **Prediction:** Who took the money orders from Esperanza's valise? *(Answers will vary.)*

Supplementary Activities

1. Literary Analysis/Characterization: Have the students add character traits to Miguel's and to Esperanza's charts. Discuss if the characters are changing.

2. Social Studies: Have the students read an article (on the Internet or in a history book or encyclopedia) about the Oklahoma dust bowl days.

3. Research: Have the students research May Day traditions in different countries.

4. Literary Analysis/Symbolism: Have the students make a list of the different things the blooming rose could symbolize in the story (a new beginning, personal history that connects Mama and Esperanza to Mexico, the thorn as problems, etc.).

5. Writing: Have the students write a paragraph about a time (s)he said something to someone and later regretted it.

Las Uvas, pp. 234-253

Everyone knows that only Miguel could have taken the money orders. Alfonso promises to repay the money. Alfonso comes for Esperanza in the middle of the day. He has had word from Miguel to meet the three o'clock bus in Bakersfield. They watch the bus unload and see Miguel and his surprise—Abuelita. Miguel has slipped her out of Mexico under the cover of darkness. He used Esperanza's money orders for the very purpose she had saved them. Before Esperanza's birthday, Miguel drives her to the foothills. The two lie on their stomachs and hear the heartbeat of the land. Esperanza feels she is soaring and seeing the land below. Soon it is Esperanza's birthday, a very different celebration than the ones of her past, but it is still a happy one. She has learned that she should never be afraid of starting over.

Vocabulary

mottled (235)	tangy (235)	rumpled (238)	deceiving (239)
escorted (240)	flushed (241)	makeshift (242)	infuriated (244)
obsessed (244)	plateau (248)	skeptically (248)	careen (249)
hovered (250)	buoyed (250)	cacophony (250)	torrent (250)
exotic (251)	infinite (251)		

Discussion Questions

1. Josefina tells Esperanza that the peaches will be sorted one piece at a time. How can students apply this to life's problems? *(Answers will vary. Solve one problem at a time. p. 235)*

2. What does Esperanza think has happened when she sees Alfonso at the shed? Is this the conclusion you would have reached if you were her? *(She thinks something is wrong with her mother. Human nature often jumps to the worst conclusions. Answers will vary. p. 236)*

3. How does Esperanza react to hearing English spoken at the bus station? How does this determination differ from her thought about learning English when she first arrived in California? *(It startles her and she hates not knowing what they are saying. She vows to learn English. Answers will vary. p. 237)*

4. How does Esperanza react to seeing Abuelita? Discuss how the author expresses Esperanza's feelings. *(She thinks she's seeing a ghost, her throat tightens, and she feels like she can't breathe. p. 239)*

5. Why does Miguel say he went for Esperanza's grandmother? Is this the real reason? *(He says he needed something to do while he waited for work. Answers will vary. p. 240)*

6. How do Mama and Abuelita greet each other? What do you think they are feeling? *(They say nothing that others can understand; they just cry and make happy exclamations. Answers will vary. p. 243)*

7. What sign does Abuelita see that makes her think things are better for her family? Is this superstition something that you would believe? Why? *(an injured bird taking flight; Answers will vary. p. 245)*

8. Why does Esperanza ask Miguel to take her to the plateau? How does this time differ from the two other times she listened for the heartbeat? *(so she can listen for the heartbeat of the land; Answers will vary. p. 248)*

9. **Prediction:** Does Esperanza eventually marry Miguel? *(Answers will vary.)*

Supplementary Activities

1. Literary Activities/Characterization: Have students complete their character charts. Do they see changes in the characters?

2. Literary Activities/Plotting: Have the students finish their plotting chart. Did they find the end of the book satisfactory?

3. Literary Activities/Symbols: Have the students finish their list of symbols.

4. Writing: Have students write about a time when they were full of hope for the future.

5. Writing: Have students write a letter from Esperanza to Marisol telling about her new life.

Post-reading Discussion Questions

1. List three adjectives that describe Esperanza as she was at the beginning of the novel. Then, list three adjectives that describe Esperanza as she was at the end of the novel. Are your adjectives different? What do the different lists say about the changes in Esperanza?

2. The beginning and the ending of the book have scenes of Esperanza listening for the heartbeat of the land with two different characters. Do Papa and Miguel have any traits in common? What are they?

3. What have you learned about change from this novel?

4. How might things have been different for Esperanza if her mother had married Tío Luis?

5. What did you learn about migrant workers from this book? What did you learn about the Depression?

6. What important lesson does Esperanza learn? How does she teach this lesson to Isabel?

7. Why doesn't Esperanza hear the heartbeat of the land when she first arrives in California?

8. What do you think Mama's life will be like in ten years?

9. Do you think Abuelita got her money from the banks in Mexico?

10. How does Esperanza's attitude toward peasants change in the story?

11. What do you think of the mysticism of the heartbeat experience, both in Mexico and in California?

12. Pam Muñoz Ryan, author of *Esperanza Rising*, said it was difficult to present both sides of the strike issue. "It would have been easy to allow the pro-strike side to dominate. I had far more knowledge about that side of the story, and Marta was such a strong character that it would have been easy to let her take over and convince the other characters." However, Ryan interviewed workers who didn't want to strike and didn't want to cause trouble, just feed their families. Through her research she was able to present both sides. Do you feel she did a fair job? Why or why not?

13. Would you change the part in the book where Miguel takes the money? Why or why not?

14. Do you think rich people share more with others than poor people share, or vice versa? Why?

15. Esperanza is the Spanish word for "hope." Why do you think the novel is called *Esperanza Rising*?

16. What have you learned about starting over?

17. Can you think of a time when you would/did start over in as drastic a way as Esperanza?

18. Would you like to move to a foreign country where you couldn't speak the language?

Post-reading Extension Activities

1. Listen to the entire novel or parts of it read by Trini Alvarado from the audiobook from Bantam Books—Audio (published in 2001, 4.5 hours, ISBN: 0807262072).

2. Read aloud from *The Journal of C. J. Jackson, a Dust Bowl Migrant, Oklahoma to California, 1935 (My Name Is America)* by William Durbin, Scholastic, 2002, to present another side of the Oklahoma migrant workers taking the jobs of Mexican immigrants.

3. Plan a tasting party of all the edible fruits and vegetables that were chapter names in the book. Items are: grapes, papayas, figs, guavas, cantaloupes, onions, almonds, plums, potatoes, avocados, asparagus, and peaches.

4. Read aloud sections from *Voices from the Fields: Children of Migrant Farmworkers Tell Their Stories*, Little, Brown, 1993. This volume includes short articles as well as poetry.

5. Replot the story by changing the characters of Tío Luis and Tío Marco.

6. Explain how the book would have changed if Marta's strikers had been successful.

7. Read Pam Muñoz Ryan's book *Rising Freedom* (1998).

8. Visit Pam Muñoz Ryan's Web site at **www.pammunozryan.com** and e-mail her your thoughts on the book.

9. Pick one chapter in the book and draw an illustration that could go before the chapter title.

10. Choose one of the two Mexican proverbs at the beginning of the book and write an essay on what it means to you. The proverbs are: "He who falls today may rise tomorrow" and "The rich person is richer when he becomes poor, than the poor person when he becomes rich."

Assessment for *Esperanza Rising*

Assessment is an ongoing process. The following ten items can be completed during the novel study. Once finished, the student and teacher will check the work. Points may be added to indicate the level of understanding.

Name _____ Date _____

Student	Teacher	
_____	_____	1. Keep a literary journal as you read the book.
_____	_____	2. Record some predictions about the book before you start to read. (See the prediction chart on page 8 of this guide.) Review your predictions as you read.
_____	_____	3. Give yourself credit for each vocabulary activity you complete.
_____	_____	4. Complete a character chart for each major character in the book. (See the character chart on page 9 of this guide.)
_____	_____	5. Who is Esperanza? Create a collage of ideas and images significant to her.
_____	_____	6. Create a plotting chart of the events in the book's plot. (See the plot graph on page 10 of this guide.)
_____	_____	7. Write a letter to the librarian giving your evaluation of this book for classroom use.
_____	_____	8. Discuss the post-reading discussion questions in this guide with a partner. Write a multi-paragraph essay on one of them.
_____	_____	9. Choose one of the extension activities in this guide to complete.
_____	_____	10. Write a review of this book utilizing several of the Spanish words used in it.

Notes